My First Counting Book has been designed to introduce pre-school children to numbers in an entertaining way.

Simple counting stories and rhymes help the child become more familiar with each number.

Simple addition and subtraction are introduced to encourage the young child's participation and understanding of numbers and the way in which they work.

ISBN 0 86112 986 5
© Brimax Books Ltd 1994. All rights reserved.
Published by Brimax Books Ltd, Newmarket, England 1994.
Printed in Spain.

My First
Counting Book

1 2 3 4 5 6 7 8 9 10

Illustrated by Gill Guile

BRIMAX • NEWMARKET • ENGLAND

Mrs Tiger, Tim and Tammy the tiger cubs, Lucas Lion, Chris Crocodile and Poll Parrot are all learning to count. They are going to count all the things they see. Try to count with them.

1

Lucas Lion is riding a rocking-horse.
He counts one rocking-horse.

Chris Crocodile has a red boat and a blue boat. Can you point to the red boat? He counts two boats.

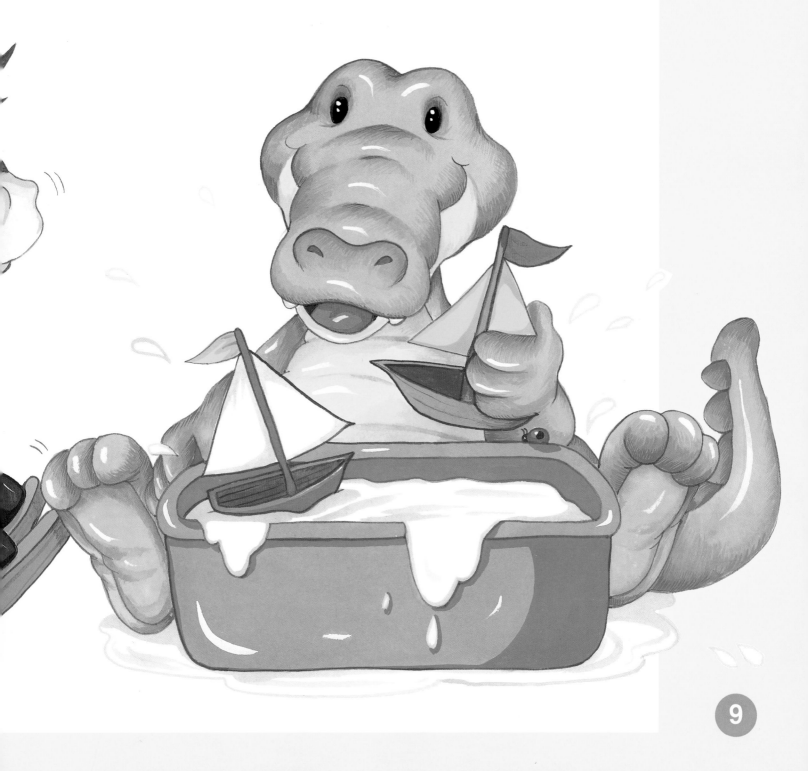

three bicycles

Mrs Tiger, Tim and Tammy each have one bicycle. Which one is Mrs Tiger riding? They count three bicycles.

Poll Parrot has some cars. She is racing them. Which one do you think is going to win? She counts four cars.

five teddy bears

Tim and Tammy have some teddy bears. They are pretending they are all on a picnic. They count five teddy bears.

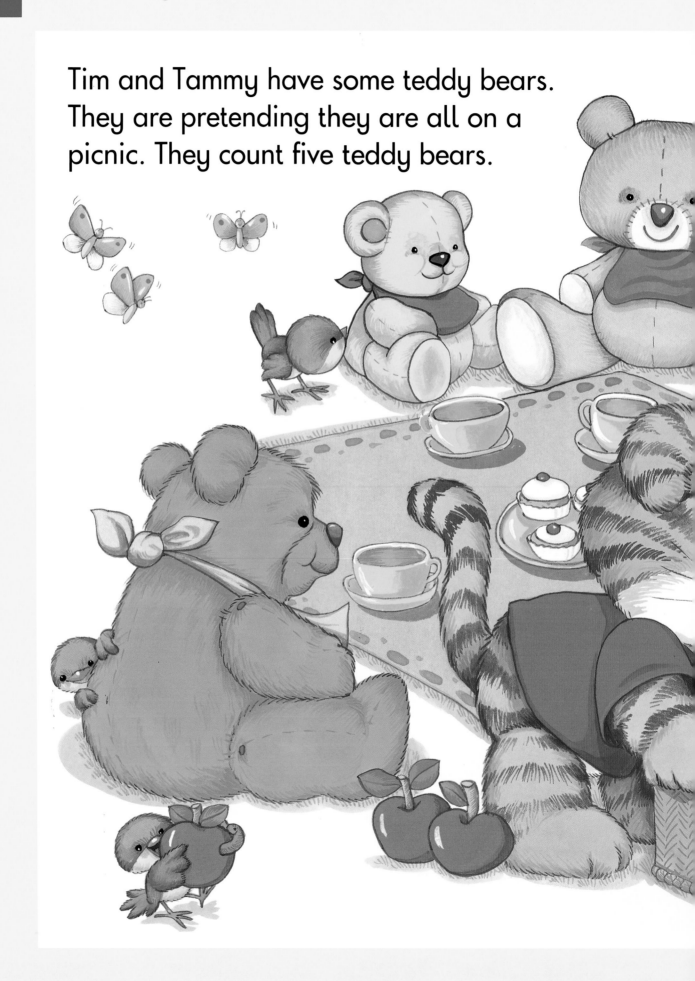

Mrs Tiger is walking Tim and Tammy to school. They are walking with Chris Crocodile, Lucas Lion and Poll Parrot. They see lots of different things which they count.

Can you count – 1 one tree
2 two horses
3 three birds
4 four flowers
5 five butterflies

One, two, three, four, five,
Once I caught a fish alive.
Six, seven, eight, nine, ten,
Then I let it go again.

Why did you let it go?
Because it bit my finger so.
Which finger did it bite?
This little finger on the right.

six umbrellas

It is raining. Mrs Tiger, Tim, Tammy, Chris Crocodile, Lucas Lion and Poll Parrot all have umbrellas. They count six umbrellas.

6

seven apples

Chris Crocodile is buying some apples. He puts them in his basket. He counts seven apples.

eight flags

Tim and Tammy are building sandcastles. They put a flag on top of each one. They count eight flags.

nine books

Poll Parrot is putting her books on a shelf.
She counts nine books.

ten socks

Lucas Lion is hanging his socks out to dry.
He counts ten socks.

Tim and Tammy are at school. Their teacher asks them to count the shapes she has drawn on the blackboard.

Can you count – 6   six circles
7   seven squares
8   eight triangles
9   nine diamonds
10   ten stars

Lucas Lion and his friends are blowing up balloons for a party. He blows up two balloons and Mrs Tiger blows up one balloon. They count three balloons.

2 + 1 = 3 (two balloons and one balloon make three balloons)

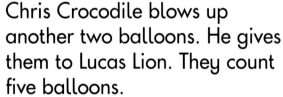

Chris Crocodile blows up another two balloons. He gives them to Lucas Lion. They count five balloons.

3 + 2 = 5 (three balloons and two balloons make five balloons)

Tim and Tammy blow up one balloon each. They count two balloons.

1 + 1 = 2 (one balloon and one balloon make two balloons)

Now Lucas Lion counts seven balloons. "Is that enough?" asks Mrs Tiger. "Not yet," says Lucas Lion.

5 + 2 = 7 (five balloons and two balloons make seven balloons)

Poll Parrot blows up two balloons. She gives them to Lucas Lion. Now Lucas counts nine balloons.

7 + 2 = 9 (seven balloons and two balloons make nine balloons)

"Just one more balloon and that will be enough," says Lucas Lion. "Here you are," says Chris Crocodile. Now they count ten balloons. Can you count up to ten?

9 + 1 = 10 (nine balloons and one balloon make ten balloons)

One, two,
Buckle my shoe;
Three, four,
Knock at the door;
Five, six,
Pick up sticks;
Seven, eight,
Lay them straight;
Nine, ten,
A big fat hen.

33

eleven kites

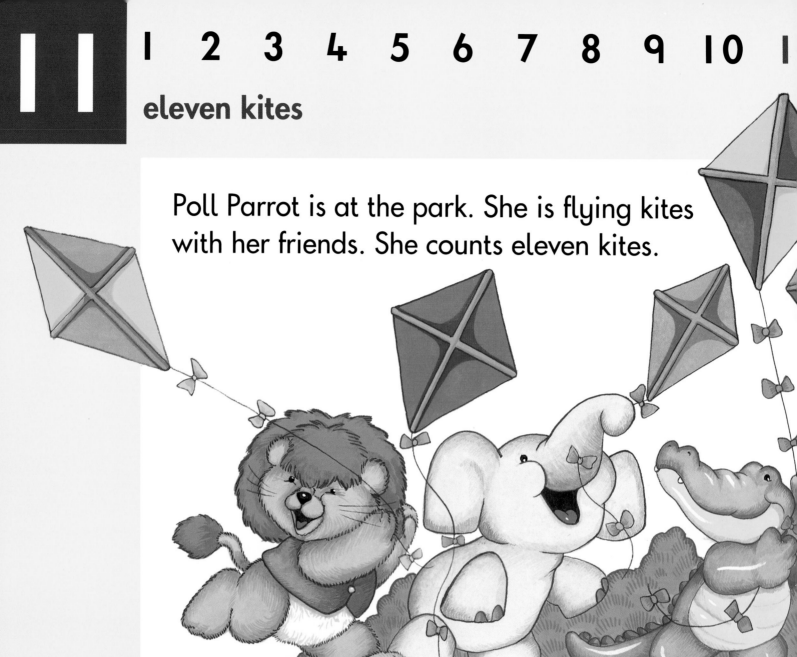

Poll Parrot is at the park. She is flying kites with her friends. She counts eleven kites.

twelve balloons

Mrs Tiger takes Tim and Tammy to the fair. They win some balloons. They count twelve balloons.

thirteen chicks

Lucas Lion is at the farm. He is feeding the chicks. He counts thirteen chicks.

Chris Crocodile is at a party. He is counting all the cards. He counts fourteen birthday cards.

14

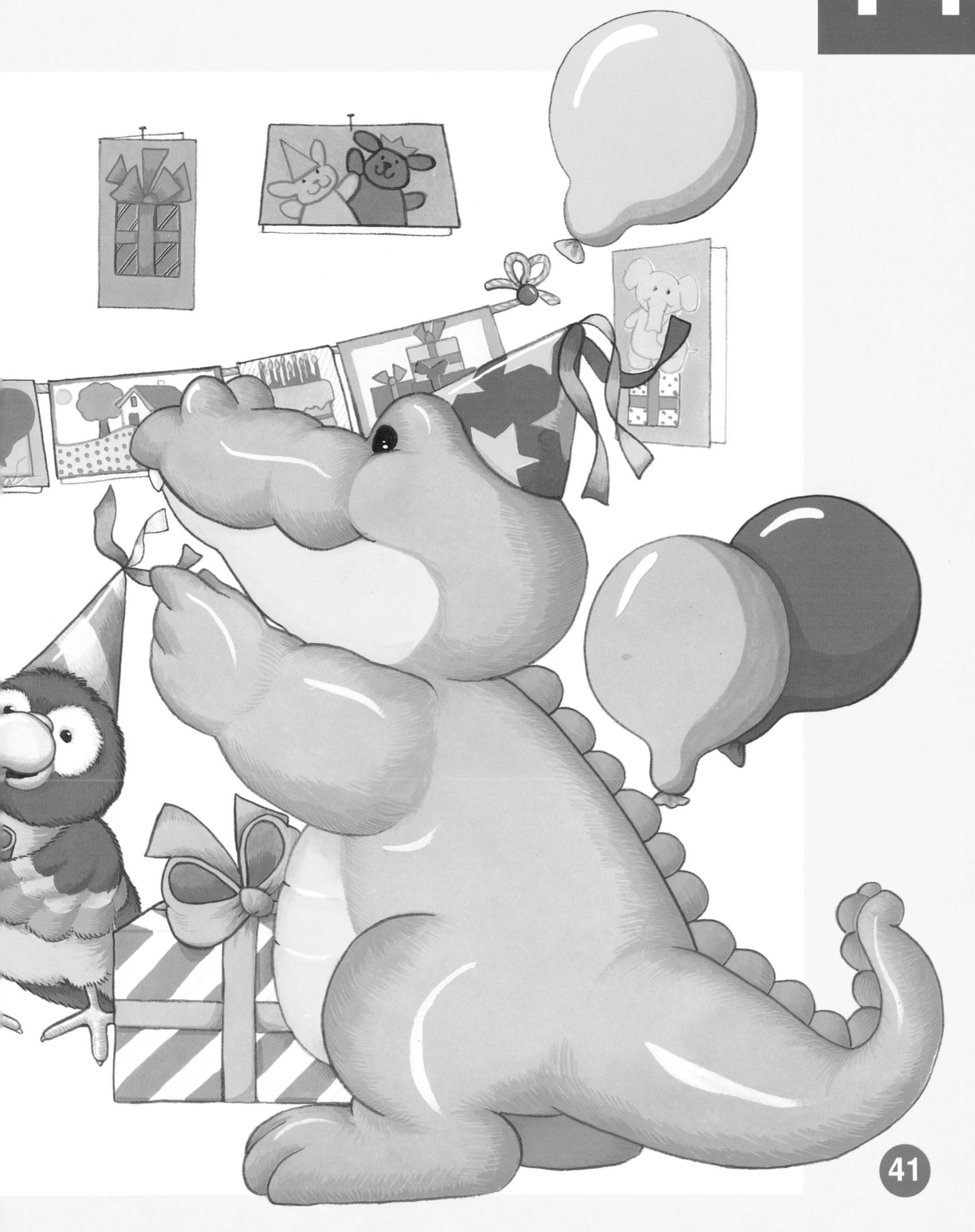

fifteen birds

Mrs Tiger is feeding the birds in her garden.
She counts fifteen birds.

Mrs Tiger takes Tim and Tammy to the park. They are counting all the things they can see.

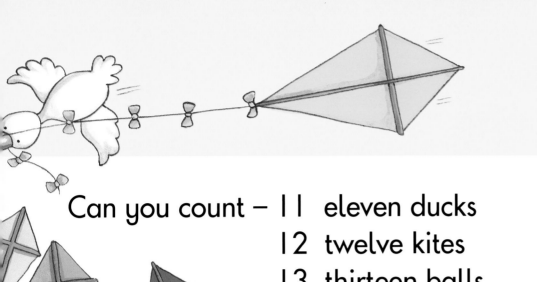

Can you count –
11 eleven ducks
12 twelve kites
13 thirteen balls
14 fourteen ice-cream cones
15 fifteen flowers

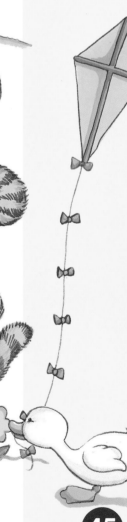

Lucas Lion is in the garden. He sees some butterflies. He counts sixteen butterflies.

16

Tim and Tammy give Mrs Tiger a big bunch of flowers. They count seventeen flowers.

eighteen balls

Mrs Tiger, Tim, Tammy, Chris Crocodile, Lucas Lion and Poll Parrot are trying to juggle with some balls. They count eighteen balls.

nineteen blocks

Mrs Tiger is tidying Tim and Tammy's bedroom. There are blocks everywhere. She counts nineteen blocks.

19

twenty stars

Tim and Tammy are ready for bed. They are counting stars through the window. They count twenty stars.

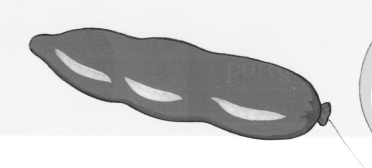

Chris Crocodile and Lucas Lion are having a party. Mrs Tiger, Tim, Tammy and Poll Parrot are there. Tim and Tammy are counting what they can see.

Can you count –
16 sixteen cherries
17 seventeen balloons
18 eighteen cards
19 nineteen cookies
20 twenty straws

Mrs Tiger makes ten cakes. She is going to give some to her friends. She keeps three of the cakes for herself. That leaves seven cakes.

10 − 3 = 7 (ten cakes take away three cakes leaves seven cakes)

Mrs Tiger gives one cake each to Tim and Tammy. "Thank you," they say. That leaves five cakes.

7 − 2 = 5 (seven cakes take away two cakes leaves five cakes)

Mrs Tiger goes to visit Chris Crocodile. She gives him one cake. That leaves four cakes.

5 − 1 = 4 (five cakes take away one cake leaves four cakes)

Mrs Tiger then goes to visit Poll Parrot. She gives her one cake. "Thank you," says Poll Parrot. That leaves three cakes.

4 – 1 = 3 (four cakes take away one cake leaves three cakes)

Mrs Tiger goes to visit Lucas Lion. She gives him two cakes. "Thank you," says Lucas Lion. That leaves one cake.

3 – 2 = 1 (three cakes take away two cakes leaves one cake)

Mrs Tiger cannot think of anyone to give the last cake to. She feels quite hungry after her walk so she eats it herself. All the cakes are gone.

1 – 1 = 0 (one cake take away one cake leaves no cakes)

Mrs Tiger, Tim, Tammy, Chris Crocodile, Lucas Lion and Poll Parrot are at the circus. They are counting everything they can see.

Can you count –

1 one ring master
2 two elephants
3 three horses
4 four sea lions
5 five monkeys
6 six acrobats
7 seven clowns
8 eight dogs
9 nine feathers
10 ten hats

11 eleven trumpets
12 twelve bow ties
13 thirteen flowers
14 fourteen stars
15 fifteen flags
16 sixteen balloons
17 seventeen custard pies
18 eighteen ice-cream cones
19 nineteen hoops
20 twenty balls